The Rising Sun & Boma

Kenneth Usongo

T0147590

Langaa Research & Publishing CIG
Mankon, Bamenda

Publisher
Langaa RPCIG
Langaa Research & Publishing Common Initiative Group
P.O. Box 902 Mankon
Bamenda
North West Region
Cameroon
Langaagrp@gmail.com
www.langaa-rpcig.net

Distributed in and outside N. America by African Books Collective
orders@africanbookscollective.com
www.africanbookcollective.com

ISBN: 9956-792-53-5

DISCLAIMER
All views expressed in this publication are those of the author and do
not necessarily reflect the views of Langaa RPCIG.

Dedication

To R.O. Usongo: An exemplary mother

Table of Contents

Preface

The plays, *The Rising Sun* and *Boma*, were first staged, under my direction and the artistic supervision of Alain Pangop, in the *Salle de Spectacle* of the University of Dschang, Cameroon, in 1998 and 1999 respectively by a fine crop of actors and actresses such as Kenneth Timti, Killian Kuma, Iris Fombajong, Gideon Afanyi, Patricia Ndutu, Perpetua Mimma, Anastasia Chioma, Irene Shu, and Comfort Tasum. Although these plays were initially performed about seventeen years ago, I have decided to put them in print mainly because of the pertinence of some of the concerns of depravity and compassion foregrounded in the plays. Thus, this drama is still as poignant as it is didactic and hilarious as it is refreshing.

While *The Rising Sun* had its grand premiere during the official launching of the 1998/99 academic year on the campus of the University of Dschang under the patronage of the Minister of Higher Education, *Boma* came to life during the cultural week of the Faculty of Letters & Social Sciences in 1999. The latter play is the brainchild of several theatre workshops that I had with members of the Performing Arts Club of the University of Dschang from 1997 to 2005. This theatre group not only animated the cultural life of the institution but also staged dramatic productions in neighbouring provinces.

Steeped in the cultural roots of the Grassfields of Cameroon, precisely the North West Region that is noted for its rich traditions, both *The Rising Sun* and *Boma* interrogate issues like moral degeneration, corruption, poor peer influence, and indolence which bedevil the university milieu in Cameroon, in particular, and the Cameroonian society, in general. At the same time, the plays problematise the intersection of tradition and modernity, articulating the tension inherent in both visions of life.

The Rising Sun

Characters

Ipah: son of Tumba & Abu Ipah
Tumba & Abu Ipah: Ipah's parents
Ticha: a primary school teacher
Akwi : Ipah's wife
Paddy: Ipah's friend
Ijang: Ipah's sister
Aseli: uncle to Ipah
Roxane: Ipah's girlfriend
Ngwa & Tchachua: Freshmen
Mende & Chi: civil servants
Abu Yerri: Akwi's mother
Quinta: Akwi's friend
Honourable: Member of Parliament
Policeman
Prison Guard

Setting of the play alternates between the village and the city.

In the Beginning

Ticha

(*Bellows*) Uooh! . . Uoooh . . . Uooooh. (*Listens and getting no response, repeats his call*)

Tumba

Hi . . . yeu . . . hi-yeu . . . hi-yeu . . .

Ticha

I have brought you good news. The plantain we have been observing for several years is ripe, from the topmost. Ipah has passed the G.C.E. exams with distinction. He had five papers.

Tumba

(*Makes a brief Akati dance to demonstrate his joy; Ticha joins him in dancing*) Who told you? How did you get the news?

Ticha

I got it from the radio just now.

Tumba

Ticha, what am I going to do now that his mother is not around? (*He frets about like a hen about to lay eggs*) Anyway, I have a calabash of palm wine in the house. (*He brings it out together with two cow horns; serves Ticha and then himself*)

Ticha

(*Inviting Tumba for a toast*) For the success of Ipah!

Tumba

How many others passed that examination?

Ticha

Very few. In the whole country, only 30% of the candidates passed. In Abebung here, only Ipah succeeded.

Tumba

What about Agweteg's son? I mean the lord of the village who does not greet people.

Ticha

He failed. Did you hear me? Only Ipah made it.

Tumba

Then the queen, Abu Etei's daughter?

Ticha

Zero. If that one passed, there would have been a 100%.

Tumba

Myself, I would have been surprised. Since when have certificates been given on the basis of . . . (*Twerks his posterior*)?

Ticha

I knew Ipah was going to succeed. Hard-work and humility can only be rewarded with success.

Tumba

What is Ipah going to do now?

Ticha

Good question. I would like him to go to the University and bring a big certificate (*Demonstrates size with hands outstretched*) that will make all of us proud.

Tumba

But, Ticha, where am I going to get money? You know that since those people collected those bags of coffee they have not given me a franc.

Ticha

We shall try to overcome that problem. We shall apply to the Abebung Trust Fund for assistance. They will readily grant us a loan, which we shall repay when Ipah gets a job.

Tumba

Eh! That thought escaped my mind. Ticha, you are Solomon. I am much obliged to you for your counsel. I was already lost about what to do concerning Ipah's situation. They are not foolish those who say that we should never cross a bridge till we reach it. Ticha, you shall be our guest in the reception that we shall give Ipah tomorrow, Ukie.

Ticha

Ipah is our child. We are all happy to see him progress. Thank you for the invitation.

Tumba

Ticha, Good night.

Ticha

(*Dancing his way out of the house*) Good night.

A few minutes later.

Abu Ipah

(*Ululating and dancing simultaneously*) Woo . euh. . . Woo . . euh .
. . Were this the moment to die, I would do so happily. Anei
Ukwai, thank you for this wonderful blessing. Who could
imagine it that Ipah will honour us thus? (*She paces about
happily*) It is lovely. I feel happy; I feel good. How shall I walk
in front of Abu Yoni, Abu Ndah, and Miriam? (*Mimics a
proud, sweeping gait*) No, not like that. Rather like this. (*Moves in
a fast, happy manner*) Oh! My sufferings are over. (*Turns to her
husband in the room*) Baa, when did Ipah say he was returning?

Tumba

(*Answering from a distance*) He talked of Iyugeng. But now that
the results are out, I expect him tonight, or tomorrow.

Abu Ipah

How I wish he were here to share in my joy!

Ijang

(*Spots Ipah from afar and runs towards him*) Brother ele . . .
Brother ele . . . (*Ijang and Abu Ipah hug Ipah several times*)

Abu Ipah

Well done, my son. I am extremely proud of you. Now, let's
see your father.

Tumba

(*Coming from his room*) Uyaka, Ipah. (*He shakes hands with him*)
Abu, you people should kill that red-crested cock tonight for
Ipah.

Ipah

Thank you, father. But darkness has already fallen. It would be better tomorrow.

Tumba

As you say. But I would like you to inform Ticha that you have come. He must be told. (*Tumba and Ipah exit; Tumba addresses Ijang*) When the cock crows, you set for Tinechung and tell your uncle, Aseli, to come here tomorrow unfailingly.

Ijang

Shall I go with Akwi?

Tumba

Yes, both of you should go.

Abu Ipah

Ijang, you go and warm some water for Ipah to bathe with when he returns. (*Ijang exits*) Can the Aselis, Akeudeus, and Mbakwas resurrect and see what their offspring are bringing home? Oh! What a lucky family I have! From Esari to Njembeng, the Aseli name is ringing. (*Dances in celebration of Ipah's success*)

Festive Moments

Tumba

My people, it is not every day that a man addresses his people, especially on an occasion of merrymaking. Such an event is rare. Often people meet to mourn the loss of a loved one. Some families have a festive moment once in their lifetime, others many times, others not at all. All depends on whether Anie Ukwai is with you or not. Today, she is with us and has made us proud of Ipah. However, I would not like to take somebody's responsibility. For what can a rubber gun do in place of a cannon? I will call on Ataa Aseli to speak.

Aseli

My children, my heart flows with joy. Shake it and joy drips from it. Joy because of the antelope that our son has caught. Adeichong, Kuta, and Anii would have all been here to celebrate with us. However, they are with us in spirit and have delegated me to express their appreciation to Ipah. Isn't that so? (*As feasting goes on, Aseli removes a drinking horn from his bag and Tumba pours mimbo into it. He walks towards the centre of the room and pours down some mimbo while making an incantation. Then, he walks towards the door and pours out more mimbo; he blows some of it on Ipah's chest and gives him the reminder to drink*) Ipah, you are now a man. You are the rock on which the family will lean. May good luck shine on you. May you bring home an elephant next time. This I say in the names of Ugiekum, Tebengka, and Ijinjing. All we wish you is success. If you hit your toe against a stone, may that stone break. (*Solicits response in mother tongue; he then stands at the threshold*) Or, if someone looks at you with bad eyes, let him be blinded. That is his own. (*Pours out wine*) Let you be the squirrel harvesting ripe

9

nuts and throwing them down to the family. Listen to your father and fortune will smile on you.

Ticha

I thank the head of this family for inviting me to share in their joy, or our joy. My words are meant for you, Ipah. Ipah, now, you are no longer Ipah of Egem, you are also Ipah of Ache. In short, you are the ambassador of the whole clan wherever you shall be. Be respectful, obedient, and turn your back to the wiles of the city. If you succeed in life, then have we succeeded too; if you fail, then have we all failed. My words are finished.

Tumba

There is something that almost escaped my mind. Ipah, this matter concerns you directly. As your parents, we shall sacrifice everything for your success. As tradition demands, we have knocked at Ndifor's door for the hand of his daughter. We expect you, upon completion of your studies, to come and take her as your wife. In the future, if you want more hens, we shall be there to provide you with them. But, we don't want you to stumble on these city girls (*Points at the audience*) that have been licked by every blowing wind.

Abu Ipah

Etaa, I suggest that we preoccupy ourselves with Ipah's studies now, not women. The issue of marriage can come later. (*At this objection, there is a brief scuffle between Abu Ipah and her husband; others intervene to calm Tumba*)

Abu Yerri

Ipah, greet me. (*Embraces him*) I don't know how to unpack my mind before this assembly. Ipah is not the child of Tumba and Abu Ipah only; he is our child. We say that all things from the river are edible. All of us pray that he should become a man and make us proud. Ipah, with God before you, everything is possible. (*She intones a religious song of appreciation that is sung by everybody*)

Ipah

I thank you all for the nice things and wishes you have extended to me. I am very happy for your love and concern. As Mama said, I think that it is premature to discuss the issue of marriage now. But 1 promise to be of good behaviour. (*Applause*)

Aseli

I thank everybody that has made this occasion successful. We thank Abaufei, Mundi, Tengu, and Andere because this gathering has ended well. Myself, I shall be the bearer of the news of this wonderful occasion to Tinechung. I wish this ear and tongue shall be able to store and relate news of this great event. (*Occasion ends with performance of traditional dances, praising the ancestors and even Ipah*)

Tribulations

A tiny threadbare room scantily furnished with two chairs. Paddy is smoking.

Paddy

Rony, we are a lucky generation, having the privilege of going to the university. You see, our parents did not have this luck. Man, we have to enjoy this opportunity. You made me laugh the other day by alluding to some stuff of tradition.

Ipah

Paddy, even though we are classmates, we perceive things differently because of our different backgrounds. As I explained to you, I must return to the village for a wife. Again, my upbringing forbids me from smoking and philandering.

Paddy

(*Drawing a long puff of smoke and wincing his eyes*) I can never be bogged down by those chains of what you call tradition. What does it serve, that tradition? Do you intimate that your parents have to choose a wife for you in spite of your education? Impossible. Did you choose spouses for them? Man, if I were you, I would smoke out those ideas from the mind.

Ipah

I can only do that at the peril of my life. Right now, I have a woman awaiting me in the village. Though I don't feel emotionally connected to her, the claws of tradition hem me.

If I had a choice, I could do otherwise by looking for a lady with whom one can battle ideas, one who can sustain a discussion on Abendong, Achebe, or Hampaté Ba. One who can relieve the tedium of marriage life.

Paddy
You keep amusing me daily. Do you know that nobody can believe what you told me the other day?

Ipah
What?

Paddy
You know. That you have never done it before.

Ipah
As I told you, I am a traditionalist, a purist. I cannot afford to break my tradition.

Paddy
What do you call that? Chastity. That is a selfish and stupid concept. I buy the Wife of Bath's idea. One must enjoy life. No pretence about it. That is why I can accommodate as many as possible. Rony, how do you feel when you see me pull along with Suzzy?

Ipah
I sympathise with you because you are ruining yourself.

Paddy
Yourself or myself? By shying away from girls and betraying signs of a social

misfit. See, Rony, there are no two ways to life. There is just one: Seize the unique occasion and enjoy. Before you there was the world. After you, there will still be the world. Do you know why these girls trail me?

Ipah
Not until you tell me.

Paddy
(*Sings a lovely romantic song*) Each of them is scheming to have a place in my sunshine. If we have them, they shall have the privilege of having partners with whom they can share experiences of life; an opportunity for them to avoid the servitude and monotony that are their lot. Failure to do so, they risk having big shots who only talk money and no ideas. (*Hesitates*) There is another side to it. You know, with these girls, one can easily validate courses. Suffice for her to visit a lecturer (*Points at the audience*) and bring us questions. Above all, these girls are objects of distraction. Once I feel bored, I walk over to one of them for amusement. Tonight, I'll be at St Thérèse. I hope you will come along for fun. You must. Catch you at 10 p.m. ok?

Ipah
(*Shakes his head in (dis)approval*)

Paddy
(*Walking out fast*) See you then.

The following day.

Paddy

I told you that you would love that place. Rony, tell me, what is your impression?

Ipah

Not a bad place. It was lovely. Particularly those dancing lights that can turn black into white. Their effervescence almost blinded me.

Paddy

I knew you would be delighted. What finally happened between you and the red one I showed you?

Ipah

(*Smiles*) You mean the one with the funny hairstyle?

Paddy

Oh yes, don't tell me you scored a victory so fast!

Ipah

She said that she would think over it.

Paddy

That's their way. Thinking over as though they intend to consult a soothsayer. They are hardly plain. When next do you meet her?

Ipah

I don't know.

Paddy

You have to meet her tomorrow and push through your dossier. Otherwise more will come her way. As I told you, this is the best way to spend life. Cracking jokes with these daughters of Eve; tickling them over bottles; is there anything more lovely?

Ipah

I did not realise that time could fly so fast. The events of yesterday look decades old.

Paddy

Come of it. I told you God created them for merriment. You know the red one is already in your net. Next Saturday, we shall go shopping for more. Same time?

Ipah

I think 8 p.m. is preferable.

Paddy

It's up to you. I bet you this trip will be more attractive, especially with *epsi* in the offing. Catch you then. (*Exeunt*)

Setting is Ipah's room: A beautifully dressed bed with a rosy bed cover over it.

Roxane

Honey, it's two months since we have been together, but you don't look serious about our relationship.

Ipah

(*Smoking and drinking*) Serious how, dear?

Roxane

(*Fondling him*) I mean, talking about sharing our life together, making a family and things like that.

Ipah

That is no problem. I thought that was already settled.

Roxane

Love, you have not proposed formally to me. How many kids do you expect us to have?

Ipah

It's up to you. Maybe six.

Roxane

Waooh! Dear. What do you intend with raising a handball team? I think three would be ideal. What do you say?

Ipah

Love, what you shall decide, I shall accept.

Roxane

When do we visit your parents? Last time, you talked of the Christmas holidays, but you did not honour that.

Ipah

Maybe the upcoming long holidays.

Roxane

(*Jumps up in elation*) You mean it, dear? That would be charming. I won't sleep a wink till that time comes. How nice it would be in the countryside; the wind whistling in our faces; and the birds chirping songs of welcome to us. Oh! It is such a beautiful dream before us.

Ipah
These pleasures both of us shall enjoy. I can imagine my mother and younger sister clasping you joyously.

Roxane
Dear, your family is very loving.

Ipah
(*Embracing her*) That I assure you. (*Curtain*)

Ipah and Roxane in the countryside. The former is warmly received while the latter is formally greeted by Ipah's parents. Tumba greets Roxane in the mother tongue, which she does not understand.

Tumba
Ipah, you are welcome home. (*To Roxane*) Big mama, whose daughter are you? (*Addressing his wife*) Abu, come here for a minute. (*Ipah and Roxane are served palm wine, roasted maize and plums by Abu Ipah. While Tumba and Abu Ipah are talking, Ipah and Roxane discuss the pleasures of the countryside. There is a mute dialogue between them, marked by gestures*)

Tumba
(*At one corner of the stage*) Abu, do you know that girl with Ipah?

Abu Ipah
No

Tumba

I fear that he is not bringing a wife to show us.

Abu Ipah

Are you are asking me? I don't know anything. Why don't you ask him yourself?

(Abu Ipah calls for Ipah and Roxane steps out to admire the moonlit night)

Tumba

Ipah, who is that girl with you?

Ipah

She is my friend.

Tumba

What do you mean friend?

Ipah

What do you understand by friend?

Tumba

Whatever you mean, tell her to go away.

Ipah

Why should she go away? What has she done wrong?

Tumba

You will not challenge my authority. Order that girl to leave.

Abu Ipah

Ipah, why don't you listen to what your father is saying?

Ipah

Why is everybody crazy about Roxanne? She shall not go anywhere.

Tumba

Ipah, don't tread on my nerves. Whom are you arguing with? I say, she must leave and with immediate effect.

Ipah

I say, she shall not.

Tumba

In that case, both of you shall leave this compound. You shall see. (*Tumba storms out in fury*)

Abu Ipah

My son, listen to us. Tell this girl to go.

Ipah

Abu, she cannot go anywhere. Except you want both of us to go.

Abu Ipah

Ipah, by the lap that carried you and the breast that fed you, send away this girl.

Ipah

You may appeal to Bunghefugho.

Abu Ipah

You insult me! (*Blows wood ash at Ipah as he hurries off the stage*)

Ipah's bedroom. Ipah is smoking and drinking.

Roxane
Rony, it appears there was an uneasy calm with your parents. What was wrong?

Ipah
Really? There was nothing wrong.

Roxane
Perhaps my observation is exaggerated. Did you talk to them about our relationship?

Ipah
Yes. They said that they would think about it.

Roxane
Dear, what about the TV set you promised buying? Looks like hell here, without anything to entertain one.

Ipah
We shall get a TV soon.

Roxane
That's what you always say, soon. Love, what about that dress you promised me?

Ipah
Love, why don't you exercise patience? One cannot do everything at once.

Roxane

You aren't serious with anything. Aren't you ashamed when you see what Paddy does to Suzzy?

Ipah

Why? Paddy is himself and I am myself.

Roxane

You keep deceiving me; you are negligent towards me and, yet, you care for other girls.

Ipah

Who? Roxane, I can't understand why you are so demanding.

Roxane

Me, demanding? What have I asked you? A mere dress and a TV set you cannot afford. I cannot accept this wretched situation.

Ipah

Why all this fuss? Why all this materialism? Why can't you be moderate?

Roxane

Ipah, you are mean.

Ipah

(*Staggers towards Roxane with a beer bottle in hand and attempts to embrace her, but she slips away from him*) Honey, you know I love you. You shall have all these things, soon. And then we shall marry. Very soon.

Roxane

You marry your beer and cigarettes. (*She exits*)

Alone in his bedroom, Ipah feels tired. He clears his eyes as though looking for someone.

Ipah

(*Yawns and stretches his body*) My mind is in a maze.

Ah! I remember a heated argument with Roxane here yesterday. But where is she?

Gone like her feminine folk in search of greener pastures. Like a bee, they savour nectar after nectar, stopping only when there is none. Why can't they be tolerant, these women? Here am I a reed in a violent tide. Abandoned am I by parents and wife. A cockroach in a gathering of hens. Where should I go?

Epiphany

Paddy in prison, lamenting his plight

Paddy
What a wretched situation in which to find oneself! Tiny room in which people are crowded like maggots. With lights shining both day and night, one has the impression that these guys don't pay light bills. Yet certain localities do not have electricity. These goddam people want to blind me with lights. (*Calls out to prison guard*) Chef . . . Chef

Prison Guard
Why are you disturbing me? You are the most stubborn prisoner that I have ever had. What is it this time?

Paddy
Chef, my ribs are broken. Please, feel for me. Chef, allow me to sleep on a small mattress to relieve the pains I am having.

Prison Guard
(*Laughs*) Ah! So you are having pains. That is the purpose of bringing you here. I am glad that the treatment is effective.

Paddy
Chef, I am really serious. Why do you mock at me? Can't you be sympathetic?

Prison Guard
Sympathy? It all depends on you.

Paddy

What do you mean?

Prison Guard

If you want to be comfortable, you shall be comfortable. If you like discomfort, you shall have it.

Paddy

Chef, have this for some wine. *(Hands him some money)*

Prison Guard

(Laughs out loudly) Woo...! I say, Sir, do you mean to insult me? What have you given me? I am sorry to tell you that I don't drink mbuh.

Paddy

Have more. *(Hands over more money to prison guard)*

Prison Guard

(Smiles) Now, you are understanding. But let me tell you that I am not alone on guard. There are two others who have to take over from me at midnight.

Paddy

I understand your problem, Chef. Have this for them *(Gives him more money)*

Prison Guard

Oga, you are the best prisoner I have been privileged to have. There are very few people like you who understand. You can bring the mattress you were talking about tomorrow. *(Extremely excited)*

Paddy

Chef, you are a nice man. This country can only be delivered by men like you.

Prison Guard

Oh yes. Sir, you are very right. I am very kind and open. There are very few people who can appreciate the good work I have been doing. You see, Oga, once you feel like taking air, you can use that back door. I keep it open only on Friday.

Paddy

You are wonderful.

Prison Guard

You see, Chief, people are very ungrateful in this country. Imagine the hard-work I have been doing for the past 15 years, yet nobody wants to recognise it. Only people like you know that we exist. Bring in the mattress anytime. A good-natured man like you should not be allowed to suffer here. I will leave the back door open for you to bring it in. Do you hear? (*Rushes out excitedly*)

Paddy

I hear you, Chef.

Interlude

Setting is school. Paddy sees results posted on the noticeboard.

Paddy

Oh! The first semester results are out. Let me see what these lecturers have given me. Grammaire Normative- 02/20. That come not go. Forbi-03/20. Even Forbi has failed me.
Littérature Post-coloniale- NV. Who told them that I was a nouveau-venu here? This is my third year in the university so I am not new. Why are these teachers so wicked? Let me see whether I have passed that "teamore" of Critique littéraire. No, this is not possible. Why do these lecturers hate me ? What have I done to them? They are jealous of me. (*In anger he tears off the results*) Foolish people.

Later in the student neighbourhood, Paddy poses as landlord.

Paddy

Yawning is dealing with me. Times are hard. (*Enter a freshman looking for a room to rent*)

Ngwa

Good morning, sir?

Paddy

Yes. Young man, what can I do for you?

Ngwa

I am a new student. I am looking for a house. Can I see the landlord of this house?

Paddy

Do you want an apartment, a room, or a studio?

Ngwa

Sir, can I discuss with the landlord if he is around?

Paddy

I am the caretaker. Looks like you are not serious. I say do you want a room or an apartment?

Ngwa

A room.

Paddy

By the way, who told you that there were vacant rooms here? Those two that you see have already been advanced for.

Ngwa

Please sir, help secure a room for me. I come from afar and I have combed the whole neighbourhood without success.

Paddy

Do you have rent for twelve months?

Ngwa

What sir? Twelve months?

Paddy

Yes, that is 120.000 francs excluding a caution fee of 15.000 francs. You look apparently honest; I can waive the caution for you.

Ngwa

I have only 60.000 francs on me. When I bring down my belongings next Monday, I will give you the remainder.

Paddy

(*Hesitates*) You see, I am only helping you. I am doing this for you because I see that you have suffered a lot. Give me the 60.000 francs.

Ngwa

What about the receipt?

Paddy

You seem to be ungrateful. You have not even paid all the rent yet you are asking for a receipt. When you next come here, ask for Jean-Pierre. Everybody knows me in the quartier. Do you hear?

Ngwa

Thank you very much, sir.

Paddy

You are welcome. (*Ngwa exits and there comes another freshman*)

Tchachua

Bonjour, monsieur?

Paddy

Bonjour, comment ça va?

Tchachua

Bien, monsieur. Je cherche une chambre à louer ?

Paddy

Tu as la chance. Il n'y a qu'une chambre qui reste. Il te faut 120.000 francs.

Tchachua

Monsieur, je n'ai que 30.000 francs pour avancer pour la chambre.

Paddy

Petit-frère, tu es pauvre. Mais, je vais t'aider. Donne les 30.000 francs et il faut apporter encore 30.000 francs dans deux jours sinon je vais donner la chambre à une autre personne.

Tchachua

Dès demain monsieur, je viendrai.

Paddy

Ça te regarde. Est-ce que je fuis ? A ton retour, il faut demander Paul-Gérard. On me connaît dans tout le quartier. Même un enfant de deux ans.

Tchachua

Grand merci, monsieur.

Paddy

Saluer ton père et ta maman.

Tchachua

Oui, monsieur. A bientôt.

Transformation

Ipah in a well-furnished office. He sits behind a huge table receiving people.

Ipah

Hello madame. Comment allez-vous?

Mende

Très bien, monsieur. Sauf le dossier d'avancement là. Ça fait un an que je cours derrière ce document.

Ipah

Ça va sortir. Mais il faut te patientée. Tu sais l'administration n'est pas pressée. Nous voulons être très prudent pour éviter les échecs.

Mende

Je te vois où ? Pendant la pause?

Ipah

Il faut m'attendre chez Katiba. Je préfère 19h.

Mende

 Pas de problème. (*Exit Mende; enter another person*)

Chi

Good day, sir.

Ipah

Mr. Chi, you are back to the capital?

Chi

Chief, can one do without? It's my monthly pilgrimage.

Ipah

Mr. Chi, I don't know why some of you like to complicate matters for themselves. You take delight in cruising here every month. As I earlier told you, this problem is entirely in your hands.

Chi

You see, Chief, that sum is too much for me. Can't we reduce it to 100?

Ipah

Chi, if you don't have work, please I am a very busy man. Can you step out so that I receive other people?

Chi

Ok, Chief. Let's settle it. Have this. (*Hands him a brown envelope*) Everything is there as we last agreed.

Ipah

Receives envelope and quickly counts the bills. Beams with joy) You see, Mr. Chi, I like guys like you that are understanding. What you have given me has to be shared –the director, the chief of service, the chef du bureau, the chef de table, the chef des plantons, and others. Check the arrears in next month's salary. Good day, Mr. Chi. (*Shakes hands with Chi*)

Chi

Good day, Chief.

Setting is the village. Tumba and Abu Ipah discuss about their son.

Tumba

I did not expect your son to have turned out a responsible man after what he did last time.

Abu Ipah

Etaa, I have always believed in him. Are you not proud to have taken the hand of Forkwa's daughter in marriage?

Tumba

Indeed, I am. Were he alive he should have got a bull from me.

Abu Ipah

You can give it to me. I'll gladly eat it on his behalf. Imagine what our son has achieved just within two years of work. A big house in Nsam, one here in Ebad, and he is erecting one in Njimafor. (*Knocking on the door. Enter Aseli*) Etaa, welcome. Come in.

Tumba

(*Upon seeing Aseli*) You appear like rain in the harmattan. Etaa, why have you abandoned us all this while?

Aseli

My son, work and ill-health. You see, that rheumatism has kept me indoors for one month.
(*Abu Ipah serves Aseli with food and then leaves*)

Tumba

It is good that you have come. I shall send word to Ayugho. A touch of his herbs on your knees will recapture your youthful agility.

Aseli

I hardly trust these young boys dealing with herbs nowadays. There are no more Ataa Ayugho, Eteiguan, or Ebarapit. Those were men who used to hold rain in the rainy season. These young people only rush after money and not the welfare of their patients.

Tumba

Ayugho is a carbon copy of his late father. Do you remember Api who suspends witches and wizards to the full glare of people?

Aseli

Who does not know him?

Tumba

Ayugho recently cured him of a fractured leg. Your rheumatic pains would be a jigger for him.

Abu Ipah

(*Coming from outside*) Etaa, how is Abu Ndah and the children?

Aseli

There were fine when I last saw them.

Abu Ipah

And Abu Mispa? I hear her husband has been beating her much these days.

Aseli

Who wouldn't? What will one not see from these book women?

Tumba

You are right. You remember what Mr. Peter's wife did last year when she boldly removed a gizzard from the pot and ate it.

Abu Ipah

Etaa, don't mention it. (*Manifests signs of disapproval by snapping her fingers over her head. Knocking from without and enter Ticha; he calls three times —Ooh! Oooohuu!*)

Tumba

(*Responds*) Eii heu, Eii heu. Come right inside.

Aseli

Eh! Ticha. I thought my death was around the corner. I have not seen you since the last two Unohs.

Ticha

Etaa Aseli, book, book, book is killing me.

Abu Ipah

Ni is right. He has been very busy these days, especially with the First School coming next month.

Ticha
That's true, Abu. When is Ipah coming?

Tumba
Abu, did he talk of Ichong or Unoh?

Abu Ipah
He mentioned Unoh. What is today? (*She recollects the days of the week*) He may come tomorrow, Ichong.

Aseli
That child is a real man. I am happy that now he is a man.

Ticha
Etaa, I knew it since his infancy. You can tell a ripe corn from its looks. I hear too that he is coming home for his traditional wedding.

Tumba
True. I thought that book had blindfolded him last time when he brought a mami-water here for a wife. I sent Abu Ipah packing home for opposing me when I chose a wife for her son.

Aseli
Have you made all arrangements with Ndifor?

Tumba
Unlike last time when he spoke through the nose, this time around things are settled. If Ipah comes tonight, then the wedding will take place tomorrow. Ticha, we shall be honoured with your presence at tomorrow's ceremony.

Ticha

Ipah is my son. I shall be there. (*Looks at his watch*) It's getting dark. Let me go and untie the goats.

Tumba

Let me come with you. I need to see Wazi about palm wine tomorrow. (*They leave*)

Enter Tumba, Abu Ipah, Aseli, Ticha, Ipah, and Akwi singing marriage songs.

Aseli

Again, I am proud and happy to address this assembly on this special day. A day that shall be long remembered in the history of Abebung. The good old book says that a man shall leave his parents and unite with his wife and the two shall become one in flesh. So today, we are witnesses to the union of Ipah and Akwi. A union that our ancestors have blessed; a union that is sure to bloom. Am I speaking on your behalf? (*Others respond Amenié*)

Abu Yerri

I can walk with my head high in the whole village. Do you know why? Because we have moulded our ridge well and now it is the planting season. Akwi that you see is a girl who has never known a man. She is one that will surely make an ideal wife. Ipah, you are a lucky man.
(*Dancing to the rhythm of a marriage song*)

Abu Ipah

Akwi and Ipah, you are both my children. I am glad that both of you have honoured us by your marriage. But remember that marriage is a bed of roses and thorns. It is give and take.

It is monkey kola and bitter kola. Some say that it is go and come. However, God says that what he has put together, let no one put asunder. Both of you should love each other and be tolerant towards one another.

Ticha

Ipah, I am glad that you did not disappoint me. Now is the time to put into practice all your theories of marriage. The tortoise knows why it hangs its bag on a short pole. Akwi now is your wife. Use her well. Be careful with the trappings of the city. Watch out the company you keep in the city. You know the city is like a mask; you hardly know its real face. To you Akwi, I have heard stories of how women have been blinded by wealth in the city. Stories of how mothers fight with their daughters over men. All in the name of money and lust. Turn your back to these temptations.

Tumba

I have nothing else to say because others have said it all. However, there is one thing which I need to remind you about. Ipah, you are the rock on which the family stands. And you, Akwi, you are our great hope, our tree to lean on.

Aseli

Ipah and Akwi, you now know that everybody here loves you and wishes you well. No person sends a child to fech for coal and releases rain on him. Be sincere with each other and Ashariakwi will bless you. Go yee into the world and multiply. (*Dancing*)

Fragmentation

Setting is Ipah's parlour.

Ipah

Darling, I told you; you would love the city. Women like you ought to be in the city where men know their value, not in the village.

Akwi

Honey, I am obliged to you. Whatever becomes of me, I shall be extremely indebted to you.

Ipah

I know that. There is the TV to entertain yourself. You have a fridge for cold drinks, a gas cooker to cook food. There is no fetching of wood here. You have all the necessities of a modern home. Moreover, it is not good for you to idle around; it will be nice that you learn some trade. What do you think?

Akwi

That would be lovely, dear. I think business is preferable.

Ipah

I don't like that. It often turns many women astray. Why don't you try computer? You see, it sells like mad nowadays.

Akwi

It is too demanding. I don't know why many men are fearful of businesswomen? Dear, do you doubt me? Please, I have always loved to do business.

Ipah

As you say. Love, I am very busy. I won't come home
tonight. We have an audit committee coming to the ministry
tomorrow. We might work late into the night.

Akwi

Ashia, dear. *Weeh*! This government work is quite challenging.
When you shall become minister, you shall have much time
to rest.

Ipah

That's right. Remember to wash those dresses in the bathtub.
(*Kisses her*)

Akwi

I will, dear. (*Exeunt*)

Paddy and Ipah meet in the latter's office in Yaoundé.

Ipah

(*Shaking hands*) Paddy, Paddy, it's a century since we last met.
Where have you been?

Paddy

I am in affairs. But for Sammy, I wouldn't have known that
you were working here. Rony, you look fine. I hope you are
making the dough here, man.

Ipah

What can one get from this public service? Instead you are
exploited daily.

Paddy

Revise your strategies and you will have what you want. So what's new?

Ipah

I am now responsible. I got married.

Paddy

To Roxane?

Ipah

No. That fellow that sucked me dry in my University days! I went back to the village where I picked an unspoiled, tender village belle.

Paddy

Rony, you keep on amusing me. It seems you have not changed. Who told you that there is still virtue in village?

Ipah

Let's be serious. The village still has its natural decency.

Paddy

Come off it. I tell you these chicks are the same everywhere. Be it in the village or in the city. No matter how it rains on a leopard, its black spots cannot be washed away. Immediately ladies hear the rustle of bank notes, they dance to the rhythm.

Ipah

Paddy, I thought that you had retired from running after women.

Paddy

They retire or I? Can they give me breathing space?

Ipah

I think that you should better settle down with one that is serious.

Paddy

(*Laughs*) Rony, unless you crack open an egg you can't tell whether it is good or rotten. I am still foraging for a serious one.

Ipah

Tell me, Paddy, what are you searching for precisely?

Paddy

When I stumble on it, I will let you know.

Ipah

How long are you in town?

Paddy

I can't tell exactly. I am trailing one big shot who wants to become wealthy overnight. It's a big deal.

Ipah

Guy, you have gone far. You had rather stopped that.

Paddy

How can I? They are the ones scrambling after me. Can you stop a bird from flying?

Ipah

Where can I meet you for dinner tonight?

Paddy

Check on me at El Blanco at 8 p.m. (*Looks at his watch*) It's time for the appointment that I told you about. We shall discuss more tonight. (*Exit Paddy*)

Akwi and Quinta meet on the road.

Akwi

Queen, business is really tough. I bought goods for 50.000 francs last month and I made a profit of only 3000 francs. What's happening?

Quinta

(*Laughs*) What do you call business? 50.000 francs? Last month, I bought goods for 5 million francs and I realised 1 million francs in profit.

Akwi

Queen, don't be joking. Where on earth do you get such sums of money?

Quinta

You will dry up here in the city if you do not have support from others.

Akwi

You mean your family?

Quinta

Akwi, you make me laugh. I mean some of the big generous gentlemen.

Akwi

And does your husband approve of this?

Quinta

You are funny. Does he need to know that? Won't he simply be happy to have a prosperous and hard-working wife?

Akwi

Che-eh! That's really bad. Where's your honour then as a woman?

Quinta

Who eats honour? I beg you, leave me that palaver. Which is better- starving yourself in the city or making use of the golden opportunities that come your way? I have lived here longer than you and I know the city realities. I tell you that you will dry up here if you don't have connections. People are just jealous of some of my friends and speak ill of them. (*Looks at her watch*) I have an appointment at the top of the hour. If you don't mind, you can come along with me.

Akwi

But, Queen, what will...?

Quinta

(*Pulls her along*) What will what?

Ipah's parlour.

Ipah

(*Calls out*) Honey, honey, Akwi, Akwi. (*Gets no reply*) What's happening here? The clothes I told her to wash are still in the bathtub. (*Notices house in an untidy situation*) Why didn't she sweep the house? Where's this lady gone to? (*He writes a note for her*). Darling, I missed you last night. I am sorry to be away tomorrow. I am going on mission to Douala. Clean up the house. See you on my return. Love. Rony. (*He looks at his watch*) It's time I went to the office.

Quinta's house.

Quinta

I need to go to the beauty shop tomorrow. This hair is already old.

Akwi

You plaited it three days ago and you say it's already old.

Quinta

I can't keep a hairstyle for more than three days. (*Knocking on the door; enter Honourable*)

Honourable

(*Kisses Quinta on the cheek*) Hello ladies. It's nice meeting you.

Quinta

Ni, this is my friend, Akwi.

Honourable

How do you do, lady? (*Kissing Akwi on the cheek*)

Akwi

(*Embarrassed*) Fine, sir.

Quinta

Any news from Ni Alfred?

Honourable

He should be coming in tomorrow. We did not have much time after the tiring budgetary session. He sends his regards to you. That you should expect him tomorrow night. (*Turning to Akwi*) What do you do in life?

Akwi

Nothing.

Quinta

Ni, she wants to take up business, but her problem is capital. (*Quinta winks at Akwi*)

Honourable

What kind of business?

Akwi

Selling foodstuff.

Honourable

(*Laughs in a sarcastic manner*) You're sure you can survive the keen competition? If you don't mind, I'll help you trade in cosmetics, jewellery, and dresses.

Quinta

Ni, that's what I have been telling her.

Honourable

I see. Queen, can you get us some drinks?

Quinta

Akwi, what do you take?

Akwi

Fanta.

Honourable

Can't you try something strong? An apothic?

Quinta

And you, Ni?

Honourable

As usual. Vin de Bordeaux.

Quinta

I knew it. (*As Quinta leaves, Honourable moves close to Akwi, who moves slowly away from him. There is some shifting movement between them*)

Honourable

You see, my dear Akwi. I am going to help you. Check me tomorrow evening at 7 p.m. in my hotel. Prestige Hotel. Room 25. Have this for taxi. (*He hands her some money and gives her a peck on the cheek. This time there is little resistance.*

Re-enter Quinta and Honourable quickly adjusts his shirt and coat. She serves both of them drinks)

Quinta
Those dresses and cutlery that I ordered have arrived. Thank God that Ni Alfred is coming so that we can clear them at the port.

Honourable
I can do that for you if he doesn't come.

Quinta
Thank you, Ni. So, what is the programme tonight?

Honourable
Let's go to Super Grill and have some roasted chicken.

Quinta
Akwi, I bet you. It's going to be lovely.

Honourable
(Looks at his watch) Can we get moving? *(Quinta leads the way, Honourable and Akwi follow suit, holding hands)*

Resolution

Ipah in his office, meditating.

Ipah

Today is tough. I have not hit the mark I had yesterday. I need to complete that house in Bastos next month, come what may. A tenant must get in there by the end of next month. (*Sudden knock at the door and enter policeman*)

Policeman

(*Identifies himself*) Mr. Ipah Agwebap, we have been monitoring you for the past three months. You are charged with corruption and abuse of office.

Ipah

(*Surprised*) Do you know what you are talking about? Perhaps, you are mistaken.

Policeman

(*He handcuffs Ipah*) This is no time for questions. You have to answer this charge at the C.I.D. (*He pulls Ipah off stage*)

Later on, Paddy and Honourable meet in a luxurious hotel.

Paddy

Honourable, how much do you want for the deal?

Honourable

Five million francs.

Paddy

Make it 10 million so that you can have a hefty sum of 20 million.

Honourable

Ok, here you are with 10 million francs, well counted, in this suitcase.

Paddy

Honourable, I suspect that somebody was monitoring you as you walked in here. You wait here at the reception and I move over to the next room to secure the money.

Honourable

Very good, my son. I trust you. Don't be long.

Paddy

I'll be back shortly. (*He disappears with the money*)

Honourable

God is really with me. With 20 million francs, I shall complete my retirement house. I am extremely fortunate to have met this kind young man. (*He looks at his watch*) What could be delaying him? But one cannot count 20 million francs in so short a time. (*Examines his watch*) It's more than an hour since he left. (*He gets up from his seat and looks round for Paddy. He does not see him. He looks again at his watch, gets up. He knocks door after door, with no sign of Paddy. He sweats profusely. He hesitates before calling Paddy's name. He calls out the name several times; getting no response, he walks off stage calling Paddy's name*)

Paddy, walking along the highway, runs into a policeman.

Paddy

One needs intelligence to fight these tough times. It's always good to shoot without missing.

Policeman

(*Noticing Paddy, he walks towards him hurriedly; he gives Paddy a military salute and then questions him*) Can I see your papers? (*After hesitating, Paddy produces a false identity card*) Ntanfan Jean-Marie. (*He peers at it*) Why isn't there a stamp on the photograph?

Paddy

It is there, mon commissaire. Examine it closely.

Policeman

Young man, you aren't smart enough. You are called Patrick Tambe. Am I right? I have been on the lookout for you all these months. (*Paddy fumbles an answer*) Mr. Patrick Tambe, you are charged with impersonation and corruption. (*He pulls out handcuffs and handcuffs Paddy*)

Paddy

Mon commissaire, this is a simple issue for us to arrange.

Policeman

Arrange what? How dare you attempt to tarnish the image of an officer of justice?

Paddy

Officer, we are one. Have 100.000 francs for your beer.

Policeman

Shut up. You recently duped an honourable gentleman of 10 million francs. (*He pulls Paddy along*)

Paddy

 We shall share it, fifty-fifty.

Policeman

What?

Paddy

You shall have five million francs.

Policeman

(*Feigning not to have heard Paddy*) Eeeh?

Paddy

5 million.

Policeman

What did you say?

Paddy

(*Speaking slowly*) 5 million.

Policeman

Pardon?

Paddy

(*Speaking slowly*) 5 million.

(*Policeman reluctantly drags Paddy off stage*)

Boma

Characters

Atandu: A village man
Abu Dinna: His wife
Dinna: Their daughter
Eberukap: An elderly rich polygamist
Thomas: Dinna's husband and plantation worker
Clara & Mispa: Dinna's classmates and friends
Boma: Rich sugar daddy
Ma Soya: Hotel Manager
Mallam: Muslim healer
Joseph: Thomas's friend and co-worker
Marie: Joseph's fiancée
The Fon: Traditional leader of the village
Town crier
Village people

Genesis

Atandu sits dejectedly in his scanty looking parlour, lamenting the starvation and poverty that have visited his compound.

Atandu

(*Legs outstretched*) I wonder what has befallen the land of our ancestors. Tinechung has always been flourishing with food and palm wine. We are even known to have been sending food to neighbouring villages. But now it seems starvation has crept into the land and installed itself in my compound. For weeks I have been living on palm wine, drinking and drinking jugs of it until my stomach feels like an inflated balloon. For how long must a man continue to live like this? (*He gets up weakly, forages his parlour, and slowly walks towards the door and calls out to his wife*) Abu Dinna, Abu Dinna, Abu . . .

Abu Dinna

(*Responding from outside the house*) Ataa, Ataa . . . I am coming.

Atandu

Abu, is there something for one to eat in this house?

Abu Dinna

See for yourself. I have told you that there is nothing. There is not even a single cocoyam left on the farm. I can't even recall the last time that this mouth of mine tasted food, not even talking about goat meat and *ndolé*.

Atandu

Why would you even remember when you thoughtlessly swallow anything which comes your way? I remember warning you to cook with moderation, some kind of stomach adjustment, but you will not listen to me.

Abu Dinna
What moderation? What is there to adjust? You talk as if you are living on a different planet.

Atandu
Shut up and listen to me. When you first came here, you were as tiny as a broomstick (*Displays his finger*). Now you are as plump as a tadpole (*Demonstrates by feeling his fingers*) and you cannot even pass through the front door with ease. Why? Because you will not allow my goats, pigs, and chickens in peace. Now that you have consumed my entire herd, what do you expect from me?

Abu Dinna
If you don't have something important to say, let me go and take care of Dinna.

Atandu
What is wrong with her?

Abu Dinna
You know that child has not eaten for a week. She has thrown up whatever little food that she had in her stomach. She is so weak that she can barely walk.

Atandu
(*Exclaiming*) *Kwifontu*! Bring her here. Let me see her. (*Abu Dinna goes to look for Dinna and Atandu entertains himself with some dregs of palm wine from a small calabash*) Weeh, which one of these problems must one first solve? Hunger or poverty?

Both of them are waging a terrible war on this compound. (*Enter Abu Dinna and Dinna, the latter holding her stomach while walking*)

Abu Dinna

See for yourself. This child is starving.

Atandu

Dinna, my daughter. Don't worry. It shall be well. Abu, give her much water to drink. That may help, you never know. Meanwhile, Abu, I am going to fetch some *atongee* leaves which you will boil and give your daughter to drink. I bet you the next morning, she shall be running and jumping all over this compound like an antelope.

Abu Dinna

Ataa, I shall do as you say provided that this child's health is restored.

Several weeks later, Atandu is drinking frothing palm wine from a cow horn with a huge jug of wine in front of him. He is eating some roasted meat and plantain from a bowl while Abu Dinna is picking beans from a large tray.

Atandu

A month ago, one would have thought that we were all going to perish in this house. But thank God that we are surviving. (*Abu Dinna smiles*) You almost drove me crazy in this house with your worries about the future. I told you that Bunghefugho could not abandon us.

Abu Dinna

Who would not have been anxious about the kind of starvation that invaded Tinechung? There was such suffering that could have been heard in heaven. Well, we thank God that the situation is now behind us. (*After some hesitation*) Ataa, I had wanted to ask you something months ago, but the problem of hunger had preoccupied my mind. Now, I don't know whether Ataa will be willing to listen to me.

Atandu

Abu, speak out. What kind of problem is confronting my wife that cannot be solved? Whatever it is, we shall both look for a solution.

Abu Dinna

Do you remember Atropen who died five years ago?

Atandu

Why won't I? Are they celebrating his death?

Abu Dinna

No. I have been thinking about how a kind-hearted person that he was.

Atandu

Oh, he was truly a great son of Tinechung! His generosity touched many hearts and even in distant lands. That man was my only true friend. (*There is a loud knock at the door*) Ingwa? Who is there? (*No reply*) The whole world seems to have decided to visit us this week. Three days ago, it was Agwe; yesterday, it was Amba; and then today. (*He calls out to his daughter*) Dinna, Iyunkeh . . .

Dinna

(*Answering from a distance*) Abaa . . . (*She rushes towards him*)

Atandu

Go and see who the person is trying to break my door. (*Dinna goes out*) Abu, what have I done that people are just streaming into this compound? Even on Ukie, when most people should be happily enjoying the comfort of their homes, especially after yesterday's heavy drinking and feasting at Iyugendong. (*Abu Dinna raises up her hands in surprise*)

Dinna

Abaa, it is that old man again.

Atandu

Which old man?

Dinna

The one who was here last week.

Atandu

Oho . . . Oho . . . Eberukap. My good friend. Let him come in. (*Dinna opens the door for Eberukap and then joins her mother in picking beans*) Eberukap, you have come well. *Aborobot.* Sit down. My house is your house.

Eberukap

Thank you, my friend. (*Addressing Abu Dinna*) Mother of the house, how is the family?

Abu Dinna

We thank God, Eberukap. Everyone is doing fine. The difficult times are now history. So, how is Abu Osie?

Eberukap
She is doing great.

Abu Dinna
And Abu Ndaweh?

Eberukap
Strong as ever.

Abu Dinna
What about Abu Igeah?

Eberukap
That one is as strong as a stone.

Abu Dinna
And Abu Labang?

Atandu
Abu, why are worrying my guest with too many questions? Why don't you pay these people a visit and see for yourself? Eberukap has travelled a long way and you should instead be thinking about what he shall eat.

Abu Dinna
I know. While you people are conversing, let me heat some food for Eberukap.

Eberukap
Mother of the house, don't worry about food. I have just eaten.

Abu Dinna

I did not ask you about that.

Atandu

(*Pours out palm wine into Eberukap's long and curved cow horn*)
Eberukap, what refreshing pleasure that you bring along! I
had been wondering how I would drink this decent *atupid*
alone.

Eberukap

(*Sniffs wine*) Whose tapping knife is this? These days, the
Achangs have been corrupting palm wine for quick money. I
don't remember the last time that I drank such wine.

Atandu

Let me tease you. Who do you think is the tapper?

Eberukap

Ajambei

Atandu

You missed it. One last chance.

Eberukap

(*After sipping half of the contents of his cow horn*) Oh ho . . . it is
Adeibong.

Atandu

This time you got it.

Eberukap

Who can forget his tapping knife? At first sip, the wine tasted
almost like Ekeino's.

Atandu

You are right. Adeibong and Ekeino almost taste alike. But Adeibong is slightly different, the sweet-bitter aftertaste that remains in the mouth is his trademark. (*Abu Dinna serves Eberukap and her husband some achu*)

Eberukap

Thank you, Abu, for thinking about my stomach.

Abu Dinna

No problem, Eberukap.

Eberukap

(*Speaking with his mouth half full of food*) It seems that *achu* were designed to be eaten in this manner. The way that *achu* runs down the throat when washed down with *atupid* is unbelievable.

Atandu

Don't mention it, Eberukap. With *achu*, you can even consume a jug of palm wine and not feel it.

Eberukap

Both of them appear to be meant for each other. The bad thing, however, is that *achu* can turn bad wine into good wine, making bad tappers look like experts.

Atandu

You are right. So, how is the lovely Engu, your last wife? I believe that your rheumatism should be over now.

Eberukap

Don't you see the way I walk? Did I tell you that Ebitoh's parents will be bringing her to me next month?

Atandu

No.

Eberukap

It is mainly for that reason that I am here. They are expecting to return with two cows, twenty goats, fifty chickens, five hundred thousand francs, among other things. You remember the little thing that I loaned you. You promised to repay me last year, but that promise did not materialise. Even last month, you pledged to return the money. That too did not happen. I did not pester you because I understand the starvation that invaded the land recently. But now things are improving and so I expect you to honour your commitment.

Atandu

Eberukap, my friend. I am very grateful for what you did to me. Without you, I don't know how I could have overcome the crisis. That money you gave me kept my family intact. You know Abu Dinna was already threatening to run to her parents if I did not provide goat meat. To imagine that my in-laws, despite their own problems, would be taking care of my family would be the loss of my manhood. I know that it is a big debt which I owe you, but I shall clear it next month.

Eberukap

As you say, my friend. In this case, I shall persuade the parents of Ebitoh to delay her coming till two months. However, beyond that date, the matter will not be in my hands.

Atandu

It shall be fine, Eberukap.

Eberukap

I count on your word, my friend. I shall immediately send my oldest son, Atoriki, to Afed to stop any preparations being made by Ebitoh's people. (*Exeunt*)

One month later.

Atandu

(*Drinking palm wine in his parlour and talking to himself*) I have been counting on the sale of my coffee and cocoa in order to pay off the money which I owe Eberukap. Instead government is saying that the price for these goods has been slashed 50 %. And it blames it on foreign debt, weather, and bad roads. We were earlier told that prices had been stabilised and now this? What am I going to do? (*Enter Abu Dinna*)

Abu Dinna

Ataa, what is wrong with you? For three days, you have refused to eat, drinking only palm wine. I never knew a man who lived on palm wine. What is wrong with you?

Atandu

Abu, I have been wondering where to get money and pay off a debt which I owe somebody.

Abu Dinna

What debt? You have never told me that you owed money to somebody.

Atandu

Where do you think that I was getting the goats and chickens which you have been eating in this house?

Abu Dinna

Your *njangi* or savings, I thought.

Atandu

Eberukap's savings, not mine.

Abu Dinna

Why did you borrow money from that wizard? Who sent you?

Atandu

You and your daughter. Without his help, would you have still been here?

Abu Dinna

We did not send you to him. You alone took the decision. Did you ask my opinion? Now that it is time for repayment, why do you ask my opinion?

Atandu

Did I seek your opinion? I am simply informing you about the situation. (*There is loud knocking on the door*) Dinna, go and see who is at the door.

Dinna

Abaa, it is that old man again.

Atandu

Which one?

Dinna

The one that walks like this (*Mimics an elderly person walking with a cane*), who was here some time ago.

Atandu

Tell him to come in. ((*As Eberukap enters the parlour, Abu Dinna, upon seeing him, walks out into an inner room with Dinna*)

Eberukap

I was already thinking that there was nobody in this house.

Atandu

Oh no. Come in, Eberukap. I was behind the house, mending a broken fence when you were knocking at the door. Sit down, Eberukap.

Eberukap

(*Looking furious and agitated*) This is no time for sitting down. We can talk while standing.

Atandu

Even if it were war, people still need to sit down and plan a strategy.

Eberukap

Let me sit down in cowardice. I thought that I did you a favour some months ago.

Atandu

And your favour shall be returned today.

Eberukap

(*Relaxed and with a faint smile on his face*) Really? (*Takes out his cow horn and hits it on the knee. Something like a cockroach jumps out of it and Atandu promptly stamps on the intrusive guest*) I am waiting for my favour to be repaid.

Atandu

(*Pours some palm wine into Eberukap's cow horn and then serves himself*) Eberukap, why are we friends? (*Calls out to Dinna*) Bring us some kola nut. (*As Dinna serves Atandu kola nut, he insists that she sit down while he and Eberukap converse. Atandu breaks the kola nut into several halves, gives a half to Eberukap, takes one himself, and hands one to Dinna. He instructs her to eat her share while he and Eberukap consume theirs*) Dinna, because you have shared in this kola nut ritual involving Eberukap and you, I declare both of you husband and wife.

Eberukap

(*Elated*) Atandu, only a dear friend like you can offer me such a lovely present. In fact, I no longer care about Ebitoh and her people.

Dinna

(*Stupefied. Then she quickly spits out the kola nut in her mouth*) No way, Abaa. I refuse. How can you do this to your own daughter? Never! I cannot accept this. (*She storms out of the parlour crying and shouting*) You this old man, get away from our house.

Eberukap

Who told you that I was old? Have you tried me? This is how they are, these women. That was the same situation with

Ujakwe. She wept continuously for weeks. Now, tell her to leave my house, she will kill somebody.

Atandu
Eberukap, your debt has been repaid. It is now up to you. I have given you my consent in this matter.

Eberukap
(*Stretches his legs in a sexually suggestive manner*) My rheumatism is now completely cured. Atandu, I am greatly indebted to you for this wonderful gesture. (*As he walks out of Atandu's house, he sings and whistles excitedly*)

A few minutes later, Abu Dinna consoles her daughter.

Abu Dinna
Don't worry, my daughter. It shall only be over my corpse that an old man fit enough to be your grandfather can marry you. No way.

Dinna
(*Sobbing*) Abu, Abaa tricked me into eating the kola nut and then said that the old man and I were husband and wife.

Abu Dinna
Iyunkeh, take my word for it. This cannot happen. Your father cannot succeed in this terrible thing that he is doing. (*As she catches sight of Atandu, she rushes towards him leaving Dinna sobbing with her head on a table*) Shame on you. How dare you exchange your daughter for money that you borrowed? And worse still, with a living corpse.

Atandu

If you have the money, give it to me. We act and not talk.

Abu Dinna

In your heart, you must know that I shall never accept this. You should better reject this possibility.

Atandu

Since when did you start taking decisions in this house? If you continue to oppose me, you shall see my true self.

Abu Dinna

Abaa, why don't you consider the feelings or emotions of our daughter?

Atandu

The way women talk . . . em . . . Do you think that I will send my daughter to a man that cannot take care of her? Eberukap has money and he is a kingmaker in Tinechung. (*There is gentle knocking on the door*) Dinna, see who is at the door. (*Dinna does not take up her head off the table, where she now moans loudly. The knocking continues at the door and Dinna walks out of the parlour*) Abu, will you open that door? (*She reluctantly opens the door and stays out talking with the visitor*) Abu, can you let in my guest?

Abu Dinna

(*Responding from outside the house*) Ataa, can you come and see who is outside here?

Atandu

(*After hesitating, he walks out and sees a young man. All three of them later walk into the house*) Young man, you are welcome.

Abu Dinna

Ataa, don't tell me that you do not recognise him.

Atandu

I don't remember having seen him. Young man, who are you?

Abu Dinna

Ataa, do you know Atropen who died five years ago?

Atandu

So what about him?

Abu Dinna

This is his son. Look at the face. A spitting image of Atropen. (*Rushing off*) Ataa, I had forgotten that I needed to see Abu Idong about the farm at Ebad. (*Addressing Thomas*) Uchie, I will see you shortly.

Thomas

Yes, Abu. Ataa, my name is Thomas.

Atandu

(*Recollecting*) That is true. I wonder why I did not take notice of the shape of your mouth. Pointed like that of your father. So, where have you been all these years, Thomas? Your late father was my very good friend.

Thomas

I live in the Coast, where I work with the C.D.C.

Atandu

You must have made much money that can buy this village.

Thomas

If you say so, Ataa. And it is better being there than here.

Atandu

So, what brings you then to the village?

Thomas

Ataa, as a boy I used to see a plantain tree growing behind your house. Over time, that tree has borne several healthy suckers. With your permission, I am asking whether I can be allowed to harvest one of those suckers to go and plant on my farm.

Atandu

Thomas, you speak exactly like your father, who was noted for his love of proverbs. I would have liked you to harvest from my farm. Unfortunately, it pains me to say that the plantain sucker that you are requesting has already been harvested. Walk around the village and if you see any plantain tree that catches your fancy, come to me and I shall assist you in harvesting it. (*Atandu sees off Thomas*)

An hour later after the departure of Thomas, Atandu and Abu Dinna engage in a conversation, in their parlour, primarily centred on Thomas.

Abu Dinna

Ataa, did Thomas tell you the reason about his coming to the village?

Atandu

Where is my part in it? When young men from the Coast come here, what else do you expect from them other than a perpetuation of the ills and tricks that they have acquired there?

Abu Dinna
Thomas looks different to me. He seems to have a clear vision about life.

Atandu
Until the wind blows, you cannot see the romp of a hen.

Abu Dinna
That young man is hard-working and trustworthy and I believe that he will make a good husband, if you ask my opinion.

Atandu
What do you mean by that statement?

Abu Dinna
He expressed to me his desire to marry our daughter, Dinna.

Atandu
What? Marry who? I cannot give my daughter to a rascal.

Abu Dinna
Who told you that he was a rascal?

Atandu
Do I need to be reminded? Don't you see the way that his trousers hang along his waistline and the tilt of his cap? I see once. You can tell ripe maize from its looks. In any case, Dinna's situation is already settled, or do you have another daughter for Thomas?

Abu Dinna

As far as I know, my daughter is single and I shall see that she is well married off.

Atandu

The lamb prowls in front of the lion thinking that they are mates. We shall see who governs in this house. (*Abu Dinna walks out dejected*)

The following day, Atandu notices the disappearance of his daughter from the house. He confronts Abu Dinna.

Atandu

(*Calling out loudly*) Abu Dinna . . . Abu Dinna . . . Where is your daughter?

Abu Dinna

(*Answering from an inner room*) So, Dinna is now my daughter? I thought that she was only yours considering that you decide her future without asking about my opinion.

Atandu

I say shut up your mouth else you won't see your farm for a week. If I hear *fing* again, then you can say that my name is not Atandu.

Abu Dinna

I don't know where she is.

Atandu

If I do not see her between now and tomorrow morning, then you will follow her wherever she is.

Abu Dinna

Ataa, I insist that I don't know where she is.

Atandu

(*Rushes towards her with a big stick and she runs out of the house*) Not know what? That madness in your head still has to be cured.

New Horizons

Thomas is alone in his moderately furnished studio as he unpacks his mind.

Thomas

I cannot believe that Atandu will dismiss my offer of marriage by instead giving his daughter to that despicable man, Eberukap. A man tottering at the edge of the grave. To imagine that Atandu will treat me with derision is lamentable in spite of what my late father did to him. If things were in the hands of Abu Dinna, I would have had Dinna's hand in marriage. And to think about how I adore this girl. (*He moans*) How can I convince the old fox, Atandu, that I will make a better husband to her daughter rather than the scheming Eberukap? (*There is a soft knock at the door*) Had things ended positively, it would have been a pleasant story today. (*More knocking*) I would have kissed goodbye to *miondo* and groundnuts, and pear and garri soaked in water. Sometimes I starve myself because of the lack of time to cook. (*More gentle knocking on the door*) Who is there? (*No response and Thomas opens the door*) Whom am I seeing? I must be dreaming. Are you a ghost or a real person?

Dinna

A real person. Not a ghost or a shadow.

Thomas

(*Embraces her and proudly carries her into the house*) My only one. Imagine that for the past hour, I have been bemoaning your love. And here you are. How did you get here?

Dinna

I ran away from the village. I could no longer live there, especially after meeting with you last time. In fact, my parents do not even know that I am here. (*She walks around his room, impressed by it*) So, this is how you guys live in the Coast. Like directors. Big radio, TV, gas cooker, and a lovely carpet on the floor. Truly, I was really missing something in the village. How nice it is to be here! (*Notices garri soaked in water in a cup*) Dear, don't tell me that you have been eating that!

Thomas

Today, I didn't have time to cook. Honey, here, we are always in a hurry. You shall see for yourself. Tell me, what would you like to cook?

Dinna

Fish and stew.

Thomas

There is some rice in the plastic bag behind the door. Let me get some fish and tomatoes from the store. The store is just across the road. I won't stay long. (*He dashes out after giving her a peck on the jaw*)

Dinna

(*Paces around the room still admiring it*) These chairs are really soft. (*Sits on them and feels them*) Really soft. Not like the cane chairs in our house. Thomas has been living like a D.O. He even has an electric grinding machine. What a lovely tea flask he has! I guess he should be frequently drinking tea like a priest. (*Enter Thomas*)

Thomas

Honey, here you are with the fish and tomatoes. (*Rushing out*) Let me inform my friends that you have come. They will all be jealous of me. (*Once more, he kisses her before leaving*)

Dinna

(*After cooking, she puts the food in dishes and places them meticulously on the table; she also puts a lovely jar of roses on the table*)

Thomas

(*Smells pleasant aroma of food as he enters the house*) Dinny, the whole compound is filled with the flavour of your cooking. (*Notices the table already set*) How fast you cook! I can't believe that you have finished cooking. What lovely roses you have on the table! Thank you, dear.

Dinna

You are welcome. That should tell how much I love you. Food was ready almost an hour ago.

Thomas

Really? Dear, I appreciate your love. My friends are excited to see you. I told them that I have graduated from being a bachelor.

Dinna

Yes, you have, my darling. Let's eat. (*She opens the dishes*)

Thomas

(*Sniffs aroma of food*) Em . . . Em . . . I am already full. (*Rubs his stomach*) I don't remember the last time that I ate such delicious food.

Dinna

Now that I am here, you will soon get tired of eating such meals.

Thomas

No way. Never. (*They spoon-feed each other amidst displays of affection. Later, Dinna clears the table*) My dear, you can't imagine how you have made my day. Do you know what respect I shall now command in the neighbourhood? Come to think of it, whenever we shall go to parties, I shall no longer be introduced as Mr. Thomas Atropen, but as Mr & Mrs Atropen. How sweet that would sound! And I am determined to make this dream come true.

Dinna

How? My dear.

Thomas

In several ways. I have big plans for you. First, I am going to send you to college. When you graduate from there, I shall go and see your parents.

Dinna

My darling, are you serious about what you are saying?

Thomas

Oh yes, I am not joking. When I set my mind on something, I achieve it. You remember when I said that I couldn't live in the village, I came straight here to the Coast. You shall soon be wearing the famous blue skirt and immaculate white shirt and thereafter you will work as a nurse in a big hospital. (*He mimics the quirks of a hospital nurse*)

Dinna

Darling, you make me drunk with joy.

Thomas

One more thing. Promise me that you shall stand by me. That you shall not be seduced by the ills of city life. You know that Uyuka is rife with prostitution, fairmania, and other forms of criminality. I don't want my darling wife to be distracted in any way.

Dinna

Dear, don't you trust me? If I can leave my parents, hundreds of kilometres away from here, how do you expect me to dishonour you and them?

Thomas

(*Pulling his ear*) I have heard you, Dinny. However, promise me that you shall stay faithful to me and listen to my word.

Dinna

My dear, there is absolutely no doubt in my mind that I shall be true to you. Who do I know? Throw me to the dogs if ever I misbehave to you. Impossible. No way. Not the daughter of Atandu. (*Snaps her fingers over her head*)

Thomas

I take your word serious. Next month, you shall start school. Tomorrow, I am going to withdraw some money from my savings in the bank to pay your school fees.

Dinna

My darling, I am overcome with excitement. I can imagine how envious Zippo, Dosia, and Lilian shall be when they shall hear that their one-time classmate shall soon be a college student. My dear, let no fear or doubt cross your mind. I promise that you will be proud of me.

Thomas

I am and shall be proud of you forever. (*They embrace warmly*)

Transitions

In a school setting, Dinna and two of her classmates talk about their school experiences.

Clara
Dinny, how did you enjoy your first day in college?

Dinna
It was fabulous. I loved everything—the buildings, the orderliness, and the attitude of the teachers. I enjoyed the Biology class and I did not want the lesson to end.

Mispa
I love the way that our English teacher articulates words. Did you hear how he pronounced the word, mayor?

Clara
He said /meə/ instead of /maiyor/.

Dinna
And even his pronunciation of the word, police, amused me. I always thought that it was pronounced /poli:s/. Listen to my teacher: /pəˈli:s/. (*All three girls giggle*)

Clara
Dinny, when did you come to town?

Dinna
Last month. Immediately after my father presented to me an old man walking like a praying mantis as a husband. (*She*

83

imitates the gait of an elderly person) I couldn't stand the shame and so I ran away from the village.

Clara
Your own husband was even better than mine. Mine was crawling like a tortoise (*She mimics the movement of a tortoise*) and didn't even have teeth. When he speaks, the Feg in his mouth can drown you (*She imitates action of a person having difficulty speaking*) He is lucky that if I didn't escape to town I would have killed him by squeezing his thing.

Mispa
Chei, Clara. Both of you have had terrible experiences in the village. Thank God that I grew up in town and was spared such an embarrassment.

Clara
Girls, where will you spend the weekend?

Mispa
I have no plans yet. Do you have something in mind?

Clara
I was thinking of Makaya. Why don't we stroll there on Saturday night at 10 p.m.? I hear that El Chic and his band will be coming to town.

Dinna
What are you girls talking about? How dare you go to such places?

Clara
Why not? What's wrong with that?

Dinna

I thought that both of you told me that you have fiancés.

Clara

What has that got to do with my going to nightclub?

Dinna

You should remain faithful to your man.

Mispa

Madam Pope. What are you talking about? Being fiancée does not interfere with my pleasure.

Dinna

Please, leave me alone. I don't want to hear about such misconduct.

Clara

(*Spots a black Mercedes car approaching them*) Oh my! That must be Mr Boma.

Mispa

Which Boma?

Clara

The one who bought us roasted fish at Atlantic Beach last weekend.

Mispa

Err . . . Err . . . I couldn't have made him out. Last time, he was driving a Turbo.

Clara

That man is stinkingly rich. And also very generous.

Boma

Hello chicks. You seemed to have left school early today.

Clara

The teachers have a staff meeting and so they let us out early today.

Boma

I see. Ladies, why don't you hop into my car for a ride home?

Clara

No problem. Girls, let's go. (*Clara and Mispa hop into the car and Dinna refuses*) Dinna, please come in.

Dinna

(*Shakes her head in denial*) Not me.

Boma

(*Talking to Dinna*) Hi babes, why are you scared? I will simply drive you to your destination.

Dinna

No, thanks.

Boma

(*Talking to Clara and Mispa, both seated comfortably in the car*) She seems weird, your friend. (*Speaking to Dinna, who is already walking away from the car*) Please, if you don't mind, I will drive you halfway and then you can walk the remaining distance since you are afraid to be seen in my car.

Dinna

(*Stoops her head and does not respond to him*)

Clara

Mr Boma, don't worry about her. Let's hurry.

Boma

I am only concerned for her safety. (*As the car drives off, both girls wave farewell to Dinna who does not wave back; Boma gently honks his car*)

Monday afternoon. School is over for the day and the girls are heading home.

Clara

Dinna, you shocked me with your strange behaviour last Friday. A Good Samaritan offered you a ride home and you turned down the offer. Isn't that awkward?

Dinna

Why won't I refuse? Do I know him?

Clara

Must you know everybody with whom you interact? I do not necessarily know Mr Boma. However, his friend is my friend. He drove me home last Friday and am I dead because he gave me a ride? You are too suspicious of people. I don't think that is fair. You make me ashamed of your behaviour sometimes.

Dinna

Ashamed of what? Of the fact that I refused to ride with a stranger?

Clara

What stranger? Didn't I say that I know him?

Dinna

That is you. We are different.

Clara

(*Notices Mr Boma driving towards them in a Jaguar car*) Dear me! That is the person about whom we have been talking. What an interesting coincidence!

Boma

Clara, it's hardly up to 10 minutes that I was thinking of you. I am driving to the governor's office for a meeting with the Minister of Higher Education. I will speedily drive both of you to your destinations before my meeting. Dinna, I hope that this time you won't refuse my gesture as you did last time.

Dinna

Why not? I do not know you.

Boma

That is not true. At least, I met with you last Friday.

Dinna

Yes, we met. However, I do not know you.

Boma

How do you get to know somebody?

Clara

(*Already seated in Mr Boma's car*) Dinna, please behave.

Boma

I almost forgot. Would you guys mind coming for dinner today at 7 p.m. at Atlantic Beach? Now that the big guns are in town, it is going to be funky.

Clara

I can't wait to come.

Boma

And you, Dinny.

Dinna

(*Firmly*) No.

Boma

(*Hands a 10.000 francs bill to Clara*) Please give that to your friend for taxi.

Clara

(*As the car slowly drives off, Clara throws the money bill towards Dinna*) Hey Dinna, I will check on you at 5 p.m. today.

Two hours later that day, Clara visits Dinna.

Clara

Girl, we are already late. Let's hurry up.

Dinna

Clara, please I don't feel like coming.

Clara

There is nothing to fear, Dinna. I shall be there with you and so you don't have to be scared of anything. I know that man.

He simply wants company, nothing more. Come to think of it. He freely gave you 10.000 francs this afternoon with no intention. You see what I mean?

Dinna
(*Reluctantly*) Yah. (*Both girls take a taxi for Atlantic Beach. While Dinna is decently dressed, Clara wears a seductive dress*)

Atlantic Beach is run by a well-preserved and richly dressed woman. Ma Soya entertains Clara and Dinna as both girls await the arrival of Mr Boma.

Ma Soya
Come in, girls. Welcome to Atlantic Beach.

Clara
We are looking for Mr Boma.

Ma Soya
Are you his guests?

Clara
Yes. Is he here?

Ma Soya
Sit down, my dear. (*She serves them roasted fish with fried plantains*) What can I offer you to drink?

Clara
33 export

Dinna
Malta Guinness

Ma Soya

(*She serves drinks to both girls*) My dear, relax and enjoy your meal. (*She notices Mr Boma, who has just walked out of his Toyota Land Cruiser. She gives him a warm embrace*) Boma, Boma, Masa Money.

Boma

(*He fidgets with the keys of his car and kisses Ma Soya on both cheeks*) That's me. Do I have some guests here?

Ma Soya

Of course. Boma and small things.

Boma

Man go do how? Do I have a choice? They won't leave me in peace. (*Notices Clara and Dinna eating*) Bon appétit mes chéries. I hope that you haven't waited too long.

Clara

Barely 30 minutes.

Ma Soya

Mr Boma, what can I offer you to drink?

Boma

Comme d'habitude. (*Turning to Dinna*) Dinny, what do you think about this place?

Dinna

It is lovely.

Boma

You are right. It is a refreshing place to while away time after a challenging day. (*Clara leaves to use the toilet and Boma converses with Dinna*) You see, Dinny, Ma Soya is a specialist in roasted fish. I have tried Monté Carlo, Pancaro, Paquita, and others, but they cannot measure up to Ma Soya. (*Takes a sip from his glass of Scottish whisky laced with tonic*)

Dinna

Really?

Boma

In Paris, their fries are rather too hard for my liking; in London, their cheese leaves a sour aftertaste in the mouth; and in New York, their hamburger is fattening.

Ma Soya

Mr Boma, here is your key. Room 11.

Boma

Thank you, Ma Soya. (*Turning to Dinna*) The German bread is bland, not as crunchy as the French. I bet you will like Spanish wine, especially the sweet mellow kind. This place is increasingly noisy. I can barely hear you. Why don't we move to a quieter place?

Dinna

What about Clara? How will she know where we are gone?

Boma

Don't worry. Ma Soya will inform her. (*Talking to the audience*) I am the boat that sails by gently, without leaving a trace. (*As both Boma and Dinna head to a different room, Boma stretches his legs and hands in a prurient manner and adjusts his belt)*

The Awakening

Thomas's house. The place is messy; unclean dishes in the sink; and dirty clothes strewn across the floor.

Thomas
(*Upon entering his house after returning from work*) Is this my house? All messy with things littered on the floor. Dinna! Dinna!

Dinna
(*Still sleeping in bed*) What is it this time?

Thomas
How can you keep the whole house turned inside out? Plates unclean. Clothes unwashed. And the carpet messy. I cannot believe what I am seeing. What have you cooked today?

Dinna
Cooked what? Did you give me food money?

Thomas
What did you do with the 10.000 francs which I gave you last Sunday? Couldn't you buy food with some of the money?

Dinna
(*In an indignant tone*) How do you expect me to still have change from the money you gave me three days ago?

Thomas

Dinna, let this school not bring trouble in this house. Let it not bring problems between you and me. Maybe I should withdraw you from it.

Dinna

School is not the issue here. You are the problem.

Thomas

What do you mean? Let me come back and still find this house in a mess. (*As soon as Thomas leaves the house, Dinna gets dressed, puts her make-up, and visits her friend*)

Clara lives in a beautifully furnished self-contained room. She is enjoying a treat while listening to sentimental music.

Clara

What is lacking in this room? Let me see. I think that next month, I should replace that tube TV set with a flat screen. (*Knocking at her door*) Is that you, Dinny? (*Opens door*) Come inside. Don't bother to take off your shoes. I still have to vacuum the carpet.

Dinna

What a splendid house that you have! Samsung fridge, dish washer, and stove. L & G microwave. My sister, you are enjoying.

Clara

Thank you. But these are basic necessities. What would you drink?

Dinna

Canned Becks. (*Clara serves her a chilled drink along with some cake*) I wish I had a room like yours.

Clara

The choice is yours. I don't understand how you still afford to live with that your Thomas. When he returns with blistered palms from cutting grass, how does he touch your soft body with his rough hands? Girl, we have to live. Remember that life is short.

Dinna

I agree with you. Here is my problem. Where would I get 40.000 francs to pay for a room?

Clara

That's easy. Have you discussed this with Mr Boma?

Dinna

No. I don't want to be too demanding.

Clara

What do you mean? Forty thousand francs is nothing to him. If you don't want to raise the issue with him, I will do so.

Dinna

Okay, my sister. I just stopped by to say hello. Let me go home and prepare some food for Oga.

Clara

It is your wretched fortune and you seem to love it.

Upon her return home, Dinna prepares food for Thomas. She places the food on the table and sits far away from him.

Thomas
(*Eating*) Dear, you won't believe it that today I was promoted to overseer.

Dinna
What does that mean?

Thomas
That I shall no longer cut grass, but supervise others as they work. Moreover, this promotion shall earn me an increment of 3.000 francs with effect from next month.

Dinna
(*In a disenchanted tone*) Good for you.

Thomas
(*Thomas moves closer to Dinna in a display of affection. On multiple occasions, as he inches towards her, she inches away from him. Exasperated, he places his hand on her shoulder, but she pushes it away*)

Dinna
Why don't you sit where you are? Places are too hot. (*She fans herself*) Besides, I am not feeling well.

Thomas
(*Lovingly*) Honey, sorry. What's the matter with you?

Dinna

I think I shall be alright after some rest. (*She climbs into the bed, leaving Thomas to clear the dishes on the table*)

Several months later. Dinna is living in a beautiful self-contained room, as lovely as that of Clara.

Dinna

Who could have believed that I could own such a splendid room? I am truly a hard-working girl. At the same time, I am indebted to my friend, Clara, and her contacts. Now I feel on top of the world. I feel good. (*She walks about proudly admiring her room*) Farewell to suffering. And welcome to the beauty of life. Now I can eat and drink whatever I like. (*She cries out as she experiences a sharp pain in her stomach*) What's wrong with my stomach? What must I have eaten? (*Reflects*) Yesterday, I ate pancake and eggs in the morning; fish stew and rice for lunch; and roasted chicken for dinner. Was anything wrong with that combination? (*She screams in pain and crawls on the floor in agony. There is continuous knocking on the door*)

Clara

Dinny, Dinny, it's me Clara. Open the door. (*Getting no response, Clara pushes open the door*) Dinny, what's wrong? Are you okay?

Dinna

(*Inaudibly*) My stomach, my stomach.

Clara

What?

Dinna

(*Points to her stomach*)

Clara

Please get up. Let's go and see Mallam.

Dinna

I cannot walk.

Clara

Don't worry. I will walk you there. (*As she leans heavily on Clara's shoulder, Dinna holds her stomach with the other hand*)

Mallam's house is fetish. On the wall are hanging different sizes of calabashes containing assorted leaves. On the floor are found several bowls housing assorted powdery substances. He also has a multi-coloured bead and cowries strewn on the mat.

Clara

(*Knocking hard on the door*) Mallam, Mallam. Open, open the door.

Mallam

Na who be that?

Clara

Mallam, na me, Clara.

Mallam

Na who?

Clara

Na me, Clara, your customer.

Mallam

(*Opens door*) Clela, kai. Na weti be di trouble?

Clara

Na my friend, Mallam. Ye belly. Ye belly.

Mallam

Ma pikin, before I start work, you go pay me 20.000 francs. You yah?

Clara

No problem, Mallam. I don hear.

Mallam

(*Speaking to Dinna*) Ma pikin, na weti wrong with you?

Dinna

(*Responding in pain*) Mallam, my belly, oh . . . my belly . . .

Mallam

No worry yah? I sabi all. I go fixam.

Clara

Mallam, helep my sister. Anything weh you do, we go pay.

Mallam

Touh touh, ma pikin. (*He casts his cowries which he observes patiently; he counts his beads; and bursts out*) Haba, haba, snake dey for yah belly. (*Both Clara and Dinna scream out in shock and disbelief*) Dat money go plenty.

Clara

Mallam, we go pay.

Mallam

(*After shaking his head in surprise of his finding*) Ya money na 50.000 francs.

Clara

No problem, Mallam.

Mallam

(*Dinna lies stretched out on a mat like a woman giving birth. Mallam performs various incantations in what seems a considerably lengthy period of time. He tugs at the snake multiple times. He visits his gourds numerous times and counts his beads many times. As he pulls at the snake, beads of sweat fall off his face. Finally, he successfully pulls out a big snake from Clara's body and quickly guides it into a gourd*) Allah dei, Allah dei, ma pikin.

Clara

Mallam, thank you plenty, plenty Mallam.

Mallam

Yawah, yawah. Ma pikin, Allah dei. I go give yuh medicine. This red one, yuh go lickam three tam wan day for wan week—morning, day tam, and night. This white wan, yuh go puttam for water any tam weh yuh wash skin. You yah fine, fine?

Dinna

Yes, Mallam.

Mallam

Anather thing bi say, no go back for dat house weh yuh di stay now. Yuh go throwee all things them wey they dey there. Na bad money weh they givam for yah, ma pikin. Habah! Habah!

Clara

(*Hands Mallam some money*) Mallam, we no sabi how for thank you.

Mallam

No problem, ma pikin. Waka fine. Mimba wati weh I don talk, yah?

Dinna & Clara

We don hear fine, fine, Mallam. (*Exeunt*)

Setting is Joseph's house.

Joseph

(*Talking to his fiancée, Marie*) When was the last time that you saw your friend Dinna?

Marie

Ever since she started seeing her Boma man, I no longer consider her my friend.

Joseph

Women can be really ungrateful. To imagine that a man sacrifices his earnings to sponsor a woman in college and be repaid with ingratitude is regrettable.

Marie

Joe, I hate it when you generalise your comments. Have I misbehaved to you like Dinna?

Joseph

Not exactly like that. Excuse my prejudice on women. (*There is knocking on the door*) Who is there? (*No response. Joseph then opens the door*) Hey Dinna, what brings you here?

Dinna

I know that you least expected my visit. Please forgive me. (*Talking to Marie*) I know that I am responsible for our strained relationship. My sister, bear with me. You will understand.

Marie

You ran away from us; nobody drove you from this house.

Dinna

I know. I am sorry about everything. (*Turning to Joseph*) Please, can you do me a favour?

Joseph

What is it?

Dinna

That you plead with Thomas to take me back as the love of his life.

Joseph

After all that you did to him?

Marie

You ran away with a sugar daddy despite all the sacrifices that Thomas made on your behalf.

Dinna

I know that I have sinned and fallen short of his grace. (*Sobbing with the head between her knees*) Please, please help me out.

Joseph

Well, we cannot behave like the cocoyam leaf that nourishes its surroundings rather than its trunk. You are my little sister and we shall take you to Thomas.

As Joseph and Marie discuss with Thomas in the latter's house, Dinna is left outside.

Joseph

Thomas, we have brought you news.

Thomas

What news? That a son of Etin has been appointed Minister?

Marie

Not that. Guess who is outside?

Joseph

Dinna, your wife, is out there.

Thomas

Did I hear wife? I don't have a wife. (*As Joseph, Marie, and Thomas discuss, Dinna penitently walks into the room and kneels before Thomas*)

103

Marie

I know that she has greatly hurt you. But, please Thomas we have all sinned and desired forgiveness.

Thomas

This is not possible. This is a girl that I weaned. Then she was as innocent as a newborn baby, but now faded like a hurricane lamp in the sunlight.

Joseph

None of us is righteous. We have all, in one way or the other, sinned. While some people have requested for forgiveness, others have borne their sins in darkness, and even to their graves. My dear wife, Marie, is not infallible.

Dinna

(*Amidst tears*) Thomas, my husband, I know that I have greatly wronged you. Like the prodigal son, I am asking for forgiveness. I was tempted by the pleasures of the city, but I pledge to be a dutiful, loyal, and faithful wife to you from now henceforth.

Thomas

(*Asking audience*) Do you believe her? Haven't you heard such talk before?

Joseph

Thomas, I am on my way to the village with Marie to celebrate our wedding. Why don't you join us in celebrating yours there? Imagine what pleasure we shall have in the village with two marriages.

Thomas

(*Gracefully raising up Dinna*). Dinna, stand up. Wipe your tears. Life is a continuous stumble. We are constantly reminded by it to always wet our clubs. (*Exeunt*)

New Beginnings

The setting is Atandu's house in the village. He is drinking palm wine and is surprised by Abu Dinna's bursts of joy from outside the house.

Atandu

I wonder why that woman is shouting outside there. One can hardly even drink one's wine in peace. It's either one thing or the other.

Abu Dinna

(*Rushing excitedly into the house*) Ataa, guess whom I have just seen? Dinna is back. Thomas too has come.

Atandu

Don't say that my death is at hand! (*Abu Dinna dashes out happily and soon returns with Dinna and Thomas*) Dinna, Dinna, do you know me?

Dinna

(*Kneeling in front of her father and crying*) Abaa, you are my father. I admit that I have wronged you. I have come to plead for your forgiveness.

Thomas

Ataa, I am to blame for her disobedience to you. Your anger should be directed at me. I am here to apologise for my misconduct to you and your family.

Atandu

My daughter, stand up. (*Lifts her up gently*) Wipe your tears. We thank God that you have come back to us alive. Your mother and I have been mourning all this while, wondering about your whereabouts. We are happy to see you. (*He embraces her*)

Dinna
I am also extremely happy to see you.

Atandu
(*Talking to Dinna*) Go and tell your mother to bring us some food.

Thomas
Ataa, as I told you last time, I shall be delighted to be part of this wonderful family. I have been praying and hoping that you will give me your blessings.

Atandu
Are you ready?

Thomas
I am. (*Hands Atandu some money in an envelope*)

Atandu
(*Overcome with joy*) Tommy, Tommy, you are now a real man. I have no doubt in my mind that you will take good care of my daughter. I am going to inform the Fon about this wedding ceremony.

Several hours later, the distinct gong and voice of the town crier can be heard throughout the village.

Town crier
(*His message is interspersed with the sound of his gong*) Sons and daughters of Tinechung. The old and the young. Men and

women. Brothers and sisters. Stop whatever you are doing now. Listen to this urgent and important message from the palace of Fon Njomaso. Today, *Ichong*, the whole village is invited to the palace. There shall be plenty of food, palm wine, and beer. Bring your cow horns and *udins*. Flush your bowels for the feast tonight. The Fon shall personally preside over two wedding ceremonies tonight. Our son, Joseph, from the Buriya family, shall wed Marie, our daughter from the Akwagah family. And our son, Thomas, from the Atropen family, shall marry our daughter, Dinna, from the Atandu family. The Fon requests all of you to attend this very important ceremony. People of Etin, I salute you. (*Exit*)

The Fon's palace is richly decorated as typical of palaces of the Grassfields of Cameroon. On the walls are huge skins of lions, panthers, and elephants. There are several plants such as the nkeng and palm fronts leaning on palace walls. The Fon is colourfully dressed in his ceremonial outfit and places his feet on ivory. On both sides of the Fon are seated two stern looking palace guards.

Atandu
(*Kneeling and then clapping his hands to greet the Fon*) Lion, leopard, elephant, king of the forest. Who protects us against the unknown and secures our welfare?

Crowd
The Fon, the Fon.

Atandu
Who led us in a victorious campaign against the warriors of Etap, crossing seven rivers to found our present land?

Crowd
The Fon, stronger than the iroko tree and mightier than the mountain. (*Ululations*)

The Fon
My people, thank you. It is not every day that we convene at the palace. When a rare event like this one happens, we have to thank Forkwa, Ijinjing, Mundi, and Abaufei for keeping watch over us. These our ancestors have made happen what we are witnessing tonight. Like our late Fon, Ufoka, presided over village matters so shall I continue to do so in his name. Isn't that so, my people? Joseph Buriya.

Joseph
Mbe!

The Fon
Stand up here, my son. To my right. Marie Akwagah.

Marie
Mbe!

The Fon
Stand beside your husband. No, not that way. To my right. Thomas Atropen.

Thomas
Mbe!

The Fon
Stand to my left. Dinna Atandu.

Dinna
Mbe!

The Fon
Stand near your husband.

Eberukap
(*Eberukap, who is seated in the audience, suddenly interrupts the Fon's speech*) No way. I cannot accept this. My money, my money. I want my money.

The Fon
(*The Fon is startled and his guards walk threateningly towards the intruder*) Who is that talking into my speech? Are you mad?

Eberukap
Mbe, it is me Eberukap and I am not mad.

The Fon
What did you say?

Eberukap
Eberukap, Mbe!

The Fon
Eberukap, are there two bulls in this village?

Eberukap
No, Mbe!

The Fon
(*Curses at him*) Ibini fain nji yie. Ajege nan chin mbap.

111

Eberukap

Yes, Mbe!

The Fon

Eberukap, are you drunk? You shall pay for this.

Eberukap

Mbe! It is the foolish goat that dances in front of the hyena. But I shall pay any penalty provided you listen to my complaint.

The Fon

Eberukap, what is your complaint about?

Eberukap

Mbe! That man there, Atandu, owes me money.

The Fon

(*Addressing Atandu*) Atandu, what do you say? Is it true that you owe him money?

Atandu

Yes, Mbe!

The Fon

How much money?

Atandu

One hundred thousand francs, Mbe!

The Fon

Do you have it?

Atandu

Yes, Mbe!

The Fon

Bring it. (*As Atandu humbly approaches the Fon to hand him the money, the latter instructs Atandu to give it to one of the palace guards*) As I was telling you people, it gives me great pleasure to unite in holy matrimony Joseph and Marie. But if somebody has come here with evil intentions, may he lose his sight. (*The Fon pours out some wine from his long cow horn at the palace entrance. He, then, pours out the remaining palm wine into the cupped hands of the bridegroom, who sips some of it and lets his bride partake of it. While the men punch the air with clenched fists in a manifestation of happiness, the women ululate while pushing out their posteriors*) Thomas and Dinna, I am extremely delighted to declare both of you husband and wife. (*The Fon repeats the same ritual which he did for Joseph and Marie*) May our ancestors increase our numbers, protect us from any danger, and ensure our health and prosperity. Do I speak for Etin? (*The ceremony ends with dancing around the newly-weds, accompanied by sirens and ululations. Exeunt*)

Glossary

Abaa: Father
Aborobot: Peace
Achu: A popular food of the people of the North West Region of Cameroon
Ajege nan chin mbap: Eater of cocoyam without vegetable
Akati: A traditional dance of Ngie people
Allah dei: God is alive
Amenié: So be it
Anei Ukwai: Goddess
Ashia: An expression of sympathy
Ataa: Father
Atongee leaves: Medicinal plant
Atupid: Palatable palm wine

Baa: Papa
Boma: Sugar daddy
Bunghefugho: One of the founders of Ngie

C.D.C. Cameroon Development Corporation
Chei: An expression of surprise
C.I.D. Criminal Investigative Department

D.O. Divisional Officer

Epsi: Stipend
Etaa: Father

Fairmania: Duping
Feg: River
Fing: Sign of trouble

115

Garri: Food made out of cassava

Haba: An exclamation of surprise
Hi . . . yeu: A form of greeting from a distance often used in the North West Region of Cameroon

Ibini fain nji yie: Let hernia attack you
Ichong: Weekday
Ingwa: Bridal dance; Who
Iyugeng: Weekday
Iyugendong: Andek market

Katiba: Club
Kwifontu: An exclamation of surprise

Makaya: Hotel
Mami-water: Mermaid
Mbe!: A title used when addressing traditional rulers in the North West Region of Cameroon
Mbuh: Palm wine
Mimbo: Palm wine
Miondo: Food made out of cassava

Ndolé: Bitter leaf soup
Ni: A title of respect in the North West Region of Cameroon
Njangi: A forum in which members make financial contributions to assist each other
Nkeng: Peace plant

Oga: Sir

St Thérese: Night club

Touh: Yes
Teamore: Challenging

Uchie: In-law
Ukie: Weekday
Unoh: Weekday
Uooh!: A form of greeting from a distance often used in the North West Region of Cameroon
Udins: Small calabashes
Uyaka: Thank you

Yawah: Okay
Yawning: Hunger